WORK ETHIC OF A SHOPPING CART SHAMAN

WORK ETHIC

of a

SHOPPING CART SHAMAN

poems

Gene Berson

HPP
Hip Pocket Press

HIP POCKET PRESS
Orinda, California
2024

ALSO BY GENE BERSON

raveling travel
(Open Book Press)

Four for My Father
(8 Mile House Press, limited edition)

Pony Express Writer
(8 Mile House Press, limited edition)

for Ruby

Published by Hip Pocket Press
5 Del Mar Court
Orinda, CA 94563
www.hippocketpress.org

This edition was produced for on-demand distribution by
lightningsource.com for Hip Pocket Press.

Cover photo: Gene Berson
Author photo: Iven Lourie
Book design: Wayne Smith
Typeset in 11 point Minion

Printed in the United States of America.

ISBN: 978-0-917658-50-1

CONTENTS

ACKNOWLEDGMENTS

Grateful acknowledgment goes to the editors of these publications where these poems first appeared:

Sisyphus
Listening to the Neighborhood
Work Ethic of the Shopping Cart Shaman
kalimba of weeds
The Old Man in the Plaza
Spiders
O Romeo
The Moon Drew a Feather Across My Bones
raveling travel
San Francisco Bay

Canary: A Literary Journal of the Environmental Crisis
River Fire
Salina, Kansas
Temporary Ongoing
An October Cricket Posts a Personals Ad
Geese
Fall Squirrels
The Seahorse
On Deck
The Troop Ship
in the mix
After Work
Timing My Breath
when we went to Ontario
The River in Late Summer

Red Fez
appearing to disappear
Constantine's Cross

California Fire & Water: A Climate Crisis Anthology
(Molly Fisk, editor)
Hard to Plan For

After Work

My father liked to sit in the backyard
next to his little plastic fountain
near the bamboo   sipping a highball
his French cuffs folded back   glowing like gardenias
following the orange satellite of his cigarette in retrograde
when he took a drag in the darkness
the night warm
the plum tree full of stars.

July 6

This is the season burs
catch shoelaces, snatch straps even
in your rubber flip-flops, work
their way between your toes with a vexing itchiness
when you merely go out to move the hose
so you come back appareled
in these little sojourners—
tough tenacious survivors
riding dry heat, spiked seeds their nest
around them, no need
for legs
before wings they catch those that move
never moving
                this is also
my mother's birthday
she loved summer
in her honor
today I'll swim below the rapids
to remember how the purling river
uncoiled the beauty of her sidestroke
a serene pleasure in her smile.

Reading the Dictionary with My Grandfather

"Read the dictionary every Saturday morning, Gene,"
my grandfather said, in his fiery crackling voice:
into this little den we'd go to buddy-up
in the apartment on Webster Street
very neat, his desk had one of those green visors on it
that bookies in old movies wore,
bookies accountants or bank tellers in westerns
their striped shirtsleeves hitched up by garters
dealing out dollars behind barred windows to outlaws
just before they were robbed—

his den had a clean green rug,
a standup lamp with a blue shade
that was a translucent picture of a lake
and we'd read the dictionary, like church.

Then he'd read me one of his latest stories,
usually a dog story (he'd been a bird-dog trainer)
a story that always moved me,
about a dog saving a boy from drowning, for example.

I liked how he talked to me as if I were an adult.
When I was nine we began a correspondence:
he'd write things like, "Nobody escapes, Gene."

I wish I had those stories and letters now.

Things we lose, and we lose everything
we have to make up
on a Saturday like this, with the fall dawn
weakening against the chill. It's a reminder
to read the dictionary
where words are found like river stones
smoothed by centuries of people talking.

Work Ethic of a Shopping Cart Shaman

"What are you going to be when you grow up?" my grandfather's neighbor asked me. As I looked up at him, it was hard to make him out. Shadows from the sycamore trees jostled his face so it constantly pulled apart and came together again like a reflection in water. This apparitional aspect disembodied his voice, as if the question were coming not from him but from the shifting leaves. "What are you going to be when you grow up?" It was a test. My answer would depend on whether or not I could discern who or what was asking.

As most kids do, I knew I was a criminal. I also had the vague sense, as I grew older, that something was coming behind me with a not altogether benign intent, a sort of psychic street sweeper, and not just toward me, but all kids. Where did this feeling come from?

Every place we loved was disappearing. Vacant lots we had tunneled through, dug forts in, our instinctive refuges into the mysterious underground, were rapidly disappearing under subdivisions, and parking lots were quickly collaring oak trees that challenged our daring to climb. The cow field, a kind of eternity, sprouting high grass in spring, redwing blackbirds nodding on wild mustard giving way in summer to meadowlarks piercing the air with jubilant high notes, had turned into Ampex Corporation. And the primeval marsh, its egrets and ducks wisely out of range, was drained and split up with levees to create acres of pink salt beds for Leslie Salt Company. An eerie Mount Fuji, a mountain of salt several stories high, glittered at the edge of the bay that was retreating farther and farther away. Wrecking yards and trailer parks had taken over its filtering wetlands, a stopover for migrating birds that no longer showed up. Grownups were assaulting wild places, the refuges where our imaginations ranged and strengthened. How can you know what you want to be if your imagination is losing the habitat where your dreams flourish?

Years later, I was stopped at the light at Shattuck Avenue and University on a Sunday morning, the streets deserted. A man was doggedly trying to push ten interconnected shopping carts diagonally across the intersection. The pavement swelled in the center into a slight rise, forcing him to push with all his strength. His soiled coat briefly shorted out in a blinding, soft explosion of sun as it rose over the East Bay hills. When the man reappeared, a wheel of the front cart had caught in a manhole cover and the cart began to teeter, tilting the cart behind it, and threatening to spiral down the chain. He struggled to hold the line upright as it twisted, like a pilot trying to keep a plane that has lost an engine from going down. But it was too much for him. Each cart was stuffed full, the incline unbalancing them. The long train of interlocked carts began to spill over until it collapsed in a clattering wave like a basket of silverware, jarring the quiet street.

As I watched this catastrophe, a former cabinet member of Clinton's administration was being interviewed on my car radio. He was talking about the role he played to create welfare reform, which resulted in Clinton signing the Personal Responsibility and Work Opportunity Reconciliation Act in 1996. "We wanted people to work," he said, "to re-instill in them the ethic of hard work that America was founded on." Within twenty years general consensus had acknowledged the welfare act added up to a messy compromise. Clinton himself described it as "Welfare reform in a bag of shit." And as for work ethic, please don't tell me pushing ten shopping carts through city streets isn't hard work.

As the politician spoke I watched this presumably homeless man unhook his carts so that he could get them back up on their wheels and reconnect them. A few other cars had shown up in the meantime, as if drawn to the scene like seagulls to a picnic, imposing a polite pressure on the man. His manner had an ironic charm, given that the whole thing was playing out in the middle of the street. It was admirable how unhurried he was, how he worked with almost ritualistic patience. The empty streets that Sunday morning allowed the intersection to emerge as a stage, an altar even, transforming the man in my mind into a shaggy shaman tending a sacrifice.

But what was being sacrificed? Perhaps the notion of getting anywhere. The train's accidental collapse had put its destination on hold and given the socially marginalized man a chance to exhibit his transformative powers. Suddenly he was useful. Traffic waited. The active world paused. When the caravan fell, it broke apart our purposeful schedules, calling our intentions into question. Isn't this why John and Yoko took to their bed in a world torn by war? Certainly Einstein's spirit would have leaped out of his grave to flicker over the shopping carts as a blessing.

Just then a plastic bag scooted over the street, swelled, lifted and escaped gravity so effortlessly the man stood there, and I, in my car, watched it flit up the side of a building, as if tapping it for weak spots, until it sailed above the rooftop and was swept out of sight. Indeed, what was the purpose of the sacrifice? And who could have predicted an angel would appear as a plastic bag, showing that you could fly free of everything you've collected and live more simply.

In another era, the shopping cart shaman might have been a herder moving his goats to another pasture, part of the essential work life takes. So much of the future depends on how we see things. This incident refocused the question about what work is: what motivated that man's work, incidentally picking up what's been thrown out by a culture working compulsively to produce even more of it—on the Sabbath no less? From what source did he receive his mission, what inspired his patience and authority, what fulfilling social function drove him and, with what caring did he lift his fallen beast back up? What, in fact, is true work?

Thinking back on this incident I invoke the angel of the plastic bag. She showed us we can fly free of our things, our stories, of what we've done and not done. I remember the leaves whispering through my grandfather's neighbor's question, "What are you going to be when you grow up?"

I felt my grandfather, in his suit and vest made of wool woven so meticulously it had the texture of fine brown sand, intricate and jewel-like, each stitch a pearl, anticipating my answer. I focused on his suit as one road I might take. I admired it but it looked so constraining, so uncomfortable. We're ruled by men in uncomfortable clothes who spend their lives in meetings. I wore Levi's, tennis-shoes, a T-shirt and ran through the marsh like Huck Finn, floated on make-shift rafts in the sloughs. But I was a badge of upbringing for my grandfather in front of his neighbor. I knew there were columns in the want ads for engineers. This was the fifties—decade of The Bomb. Math and

Science were the power and way. "An engineer," I answered. I heard my voice thin. I was lying. And the two men were complicit. I liked to go barefoot and was beginning to resent the regimentation of school. Huck Finn had caught my imagination on fire and I had my own way to go. But I had to keep it to myself, at least for the time being. As Huck had said when he escaped Aunt Polly's that night, out the window and over the roof to shimmy down the tree to make for his raft, it had been a close call. He was starting to like wearing shoes. He was getting to like being civilized. But Jim needed his help.

It's vital that we struggle to do what we want to do. Our dreams are often casualties of growing up. What happens to them? The answer is in the streets. People are pushing shopping carts through our cities' back alleys looking for the dreams we threw away when we grew up and took jobs we hated. As a culture we are living an unimagined life. We are destroying the habitat of our imagination.

when we went to Ontario
for Ruby

we often saw Adirondack chairs
at the end of a pier that extended far
into lake after lake

they didn't make you feel sad exactly
they were kind of a blues note
that stirred a yearning
for another life or for something
that may never be

sometimes two people
would be sitting there
looking out on the lake
not saying anything

but mostly there were just
the chairs at the end of the pier
then the lake
and the changing light

the chairs were waiting
people not making it down to the water
as often anymore
sometimes only one   angled
to suggest the favorite perspective of a spouse
who had become part of the view

it seems irrefutable that we die alone
even after a long life together
but those chairs made you
uncertain   uncertain about everything
as if everything were poised
boulders in a boulder field

their tumbling visible but arrested
suspended in a kind of waiting
for something
that is happening but not happening
or something that never quite happens
while you're looking
or has already happened
in the transitioning air

we drove by each lake
piers carrying chairs would float into view
glide along the side window
slightly more slowly
than cars we were passing
contract in the mirror
and disappear

to then beckon us from memory
their solitariness corresponding to our own
almost afflicting us with their forlorn being
tempting us
not to leave them behind

but it had to be
like forcing young to fend for themselves
we knew we couldn't yield to their call
we had to leave
or we'd never be able to keep going
through those birch forests
that got shorter
and shorter as we drove
toward the top of the world

the chairs made us feel
we were leaving home
and might or might not
someday return but
strangely   neither of us
had ever been there before

and we were on our way
as I say
to the top of the world

we wanted to say goodbye
to the polar bears

Constantine's Cross

"In hoc signo vinces," I read out loud
then translated for my friends:
"In this sign you will conquer"
from the crest on the red pack of Pall Malls
we all smoked.

Sitting in the back of Joel Anderson's '51 Ford
cutting class again, the probable dropouts,
the troubled delinquents, the ones
teachers no longer even looked at.

my friends eyed me somewhat stunned
as if I were some sort of magician.

"Per aspera ad astra," I went on.
Kroner was blowing smoke rings like jellyfish
pulsing toward the headliner, the wavering
coherent circles propelled
upward to splash silently
against the dark interior,
the cirrus web stretched and thinned—
it was David's finest accomplishment.

"Through hope to the stars," I translated.

"Fuck school," Giannouni said softly.
"Let's go to the ocean," someone chimed.
"Anybody got any gas money?"

We filled up at the 29-cents-a-gallon station near Jiffy Burgers
laughed and fucked off the whole day.

Coming back we took Sneath Lane
past blinking crosses of the VA cemetery
glowing under the overcast sky of San Bruno.

When Dougie was killed in Vietnam a few years later
people heading back to their cars after the funeral
I wandered through the graves a while
reading inscriptions. Different wars
but most dates carved into the stones marked
the remains of seventeen-to-twenty-two-year-olds.

We ended up shooting pool
in the back of Herb & Jim's Smoke Shop on Main Street.
Padilla broke the rack
so hard the crackling fusillade
may have furrowed even God's brow
as balls slowed on the felt
to a final click.

Henry set his cigarette on the edge
burn marks there before him
chalked his cue stick
moved around the table
all eyes on him.

As he lined up his shot
his gold cross swung beneath his throat
glinting in the smoke.

The Wanderer

I was flunking out of high school
and rarely went to class
Mornings found me
in the back of Roger's '49 Olds
or Kenny Moots' black primer '48 Ford
in the school parking lot
smoking Pall Malls with three or four guys
misfits out of two thousand kids
listening to Ray Charles on KDIA

One day I went to English class
I don't know why
and was surprised because
it was library day
We pushed down the corridors
past the hospital-green poles
into the library
to find our books
animals released into an enforced quiet
ducking the librarians' wary glances
as we walked among the shelves
to pick a book
any book we were told
for an oral report

I loved the feeling in the room
kids moving past each other
as if in a trance of being ignorant
Most went for the thinnest books
but I took my time
weighing all the titles within myself
until I found it the book meant for me

The Wanderer
by Mika Waltari

It was set during the Crusades
about a European passenger on a ship
taken over by Arab pirates
Everyone on board was given the option
of joining Islam or having his head cut off
There were those who chose death
rather than betray their faith
heads and bodies flung into the sea
For them, the book was over
One man converted easily a doctor I liked
because he was always
secretly observing things like I did
and who didn't really care about being Catholic
What was loyalty anyway
What should you be loyal to
Loyalty to one thing
betrayed another
like seeing two friends fighting
I often saw both sides
Class wisdom said let them fight it out
but in the case of religion
I felt up against a sort of coerced belief
versus the more tolerant curiosity
that was natural to me I began to sense
some danger in my reservations to take sides
but also a chance to be free
but of what exactly I wasn't sure yet

After his conversion
the doctor was brought to Africa
still herded about but
mostly ignored just like I was
Eventually his doctoring skills came to light
A sultan took a liking to him
and he ended up a royal physician
who could walk around in sunlit courtyards
think   notice the different African birds
practice his Arabic
There were moments of danger and crisis

which he skillfully navigated
not being too attached to what he was
He was beyond being European or Arab
a wanderer adjusting to how people saw him
playing with appearances
like fish do hiding beneath their own reflections
He was what my mother called an opportunist
a corrupt person without character or core beliefs
She often called me an opportunist which I resented
because of the grain of truth it contained
"And you never finish anything"
Of course I rarely did finish anything
But her vehemence puzzled me
Her firm betrayed eyes
beseeched me ordered me dared me even
from within her marvelous reserve
to be her ally in a cause I didn't understand

When I got up to give my report
all the kids looked at me
curious because I had never participated
in anything before
The girls looked like they felt sorry for me
I laid out how I really liked the doctor
who made every decision
without regard for any imposed belief
religion or country or whatever
exposing them as the illusions they really were
"You might think this guy's a two-faced
opportunist but he really isn't
He understood you could be killed
according to how people see you
and wasn't beyond putting up appearances" I said
standing up for myself

After the report you had to go over
to Mrs. Weiner to quietly huddle up with her
and get a grade on your report
while some other kid was getting ready

I was beyond grades by that time
But the intimacy excited me
I felt that I had done all right
because I had gotten carried away
and felt part of the class for once
even though it was too late

I remember Mrs. Weiner's
pellucid brown eyes holding mine
"Gene it would be a real shame
if you never went to college" she said
College of course was out of the question for me
but for the first time I felt seen
compassionately understood
in the argument I was having with myself
and remember her warmly to this day

After class a girl who never spoke to me before
with mesmerizing blue eyes, came up and said,
If you quit high school
you'll end up pumping gas your whole life
Her glacial blue eyes
promised another world
so far away you could never reach it
and if you did
you would never make it back

You'll pump gas your whole life!
I liked how directly she said it
She was really trying to talk to me
even though we came from different worlds
She drove a new Corvette and I knew
she'd never go out with me
or any of my friends in a million years
She was really talking to me about her own fears
of straying too far off the path to success
I heard some adult in her voice probably her father
trying to scare her
She decided to be good

as I decided to be bad
We shared the experience of those decisions
and looked at each other
across a widening river

Somehow I wasn't scared
in the way my classmates were
I watched them
cutting each other off to get out the door
as if scrambling toward a cliff
I didn't know how to tell them was there

Song of a High School Dropout

I read matchbook covers
My mother cried when I quit
I'm in a streetcar tunnel
Riding along, riding alone
Watching my face, my face
Filmed in a related journey.
I see my face that sees me.

When I quit it was raining
I needed the Dean's signature.
I crossed, recrossed my legs:
Waited. He wouldn't look up.
I watched his thinning hair
While he wrote; while he wrote
Blinds clinked lightly behind him.

Outside, wind blew into a tree
And undid her hair in streams

Salina, Kansas

I couldn't get a ride out of town
I couldn't get a ride
back into town, and it was cold

getting dark
so I went into a wrecking yard
crawled into the back seat
of a '39 Chevy

when I opened my eyes
a caravan of dew
was crossing a velvet terrain
back of the old front seat
each drop quivering under its burden
of morning sun

I now realize how rare it is to see
that caravan from afar
apart from it
lying in the back of an old car
in a wrecking yard in Kansas
in winter
without a dollar in your pocket

it came with a feeling of happiness
being solitary, able to watch
each wobbling dewdrop
carry its sack of sunlight
across that old velvet seat

when I finally got a ride
from a farmer and his wife
we were quiet
listening to the tires
it felt familiar between us, as if we were
the only people in the world
who knew each other

I was glad for the heater
and watched the passing fields
thinking how different it was
when you were out in it, prairie wind
came off the snow in sharp points
froze the moisture from your breath
on the fur around your parka hood
numbed your fingers
when you pulled them from your mittens
before you could get your canteen out

but from the car
the wintry landscape went by
like a movie, on its own,
birds distant specks
scattered across white sky

that severe cold was new to me
when you were out in it
but had a kind of absolving beauty to it
from the warm car

"Where you from, son?" the man asked.
He had a healthy redness to his cheeks
and strong fingers that guided the wheel gently.

"California," I said.
"Bit different here, hunh?" he said,
giving me a slight smile.

"Yeah," I answered. "So flat, without trees.
I felt a little trapped at first,
being so far from the ocean. But now
looking across it is starting to give me the same feeling
I used to get looking at the sea."

"I remember when I first saw the ocean,
on the ship overseas." he said. "I was mostly scared,
but everything got wider." His wife in the back

didn't say anything, just letting things be,
seemed to hold us together somehow.
We listened to the tires some more.

"I got a Eisenhower jacket," the farmer
continued softly, laugh lines radiating fine spokes
at the corners of his eyes, "Hangin'
in the closet, one a them Big Red One
patches on the shoulder."

His war was over of course;
however, it might've still been playing
inside him, but we both knew another war,
initially rumored to be Laos,
was coming.

"What's your MOS, son?"
"I'm a radio operator," I said,
"in a rifle platoon."
"That damned radio," he said.
His comment surprised me
but said a lot. "Yeah," I said
thinking of how heavy it got
pressing on your back all the time
along with all the other stuff you had to carry.

"'Specially when you have to run," the farmer said.

His eyes passed something into mine,
a cartridge of grateful sorrow
locked into the breach of time.

Neither of us realized it was already too late
for a repeat, the illusion
of fighting for your country
as in WWII, was already obsolete, incense
and draft cards about to be lit.

At the DMZ

The army told us we were on *Freedom's Frontier*
but I was a kid on a hill halfway around the world.
Korea's fabled medieval forests had been stripped
by forty-four years of Japanese occupation,
the Korean war, and ten years of erosion.
Firewood was precious, most villages without power.

Korean women climbed out of the valley
body heat swelling cotton clothing cinched at wrist
and ankle against the January wind
to where I sat alone on frozen ground
maintaining radio contact, listening
to the river in the headset, 106's
firing idiotically over the knoll, jarring the quiet
for weapons platoon practice—the women came
to collect firewood from the ammo boxes, looked at me
to make sure I didn't mind, then seeing me nod,
went ahead and broke down the boxes
and loaded them on the A-frames they carried on their backs,
built a fire with scraps they had set aside and squatted around the fire,
over twenty women of various ages, and turned
as they got comfortable, one after the other
their brown beaming faces, and giggled
shyly beckoning me over to warm up.
Yes, close to the DMZ those women
squeezed me in among them around that fire
on an empty freezing hill, guns going off out of sight
as we did our best in a language I barely understood
warmth translating every word
the radio crackling in the snowbank
between explosions.

The Troop Ship

I found myself on a folding metal chair
at an environmental film festival
with a few dozen people
in an echoing junior high gymnasium
wind and rain slashing the high windows

on the screen a biologist
a woman with the bravery
stamina and love it takes
to look at things as they are
spreads the belly feathers of a dead albatross
stretches its intestines to reveal
the red bottlecap that killed it
in a nest of bones

the movie ends soon after, credits scroll
people get up, pull on their coats,
avoid looking at each other

once outside, grateful for the cold air
I walk down the hill toward Main Street

this is an old gold-mining town
second story iron shutters and ghosts
to be reckoned with as this town makes do
with aging back-to-the-landers
environmental and recreational tourists
artists organic farmers real estate people retirees
all facing longer fire seasons every year

up the street a black oak in the mist
looks like a silent figure about to depart
people fill the sidewalks cross the street
check film catalogues and venue maps
on their way to the next film

the rain has stopped pieces of sky
lie shattered in puddles
cars pass over the tacky street
as if someone were slowly tearing pages
out of the newspaper

I get a black tea at the cafe
sweep raindrops off an outside bench
squeeze the lid off
a flat scarf of steam twists and disappears
into the cold air the tea tastes clean and bitter
and I'm glad for it
after that movie

I'm thankful for those who made the film
for its sobering effect
and the softness it caused in me
what it made me remember again
after so many years

we slept in the second hold
deep amidship
racks of four or five fold-down hammocks
hundreds of them taut canvas
laced to steel frames hinged to a pole
you could sling your arm around
to keep from rolling off
as the giant ship rocked like a toy
in the Pacific

one night the storm was so insistent
I got up the other soldiers sleeping
throughout the bay breathing
as if part of the rocking ship
made my way over the riveted floor
through the angled latrine toward the fantail
all the heads gleaming silent and bizarre
and out the steel door

I emerged into sweet ocean air
the sea rose up like a mountain
night blue galaxies of luminous foam
loosening on the wave
the air so alive I felt pulled through my own skin

albatross circled without a wingbeat
softly threading every nuance of air
days from land prehistorically patient
for the galley scraps we tossed overboard
I stood there watching them silently sweep
up and out of sight as if they were shadows
lifted off the surface of the water
to circle back into view and pass through me
so at home on their wings.

On Deck

The boatload of Libyan refugees
who had hoped to escape merciless slaughter
were drowned, perhaps on purpose
—eighteen-year-olds
desperately fleeing to live.

Dawn revealed
their bodies, floating apart, stiff arms reaching
on the reliable tide, the previous day's screams
replaced by a sky full of excited gulls.

I turn off the TV, go outside
start sweeping leaves from the deck
layered six inches thick
crisp as potato chips.
Heavy rains this spring, double the average
caused a mold so the oak leaves
are dropping early, stressing the trees
to put out a second wave of leaves in one season.

Barely August, the black oaks
are releasing a slow-motion fountain of leaves
showering shadows over a meadow of wild peas.
Pods twist open
a fusillade of seeds
crackles like a wicker chair
as if the wary rear end of a favorite aunt
were settling into it. Indeed it is hot
and we all know it is hotter than it should be.
Please bring Mother Earth a glass of iced tea.

Watering the deck plants
I surprise a little frog
that spurts from the fern
sticks to the wall, terrified,

hoping he's not seen,
depending on human tenderness.

A truant breeze
ripples through the wind chimes.
Those refugees' cries, strangled by water,
subsided in the sparkling sea.

The little frog is hiding
in stillness, in plain sight
against the wall.
Neither of us is kidding himself.

beautiful husks

stopped at the signal
watching weeds
fill with light
barley swaying
empty lanterns
the overpass vibrating
setting sun angled in
between concrete supports
the sorrow beauty can cause in you
so empty
light shines through
from childhood
the cow field
breezes off the bay unrolling
shadows through hay like a scroll
sprouted up through a crack
next to a freeway support
a man huddled against it
hidden in a blanket
covered with light
while I wait for the signal
to click stopped
in my tracks stunned
by glowing husks as if
to say here's a bouquet
of empty weeds
to sip sunlight through
while you wait

Point of View

William F. Buckley is interviewing Muhammad Ali
on YouTube. Buckley snidely reveals his rat-tooth smile,
interrogates Ali with polysyllabic words
as if he were setting out traps. Ali looks at him
in a calm, unwavering assessment, then says,
"I've only got a high school education
and don't know what them words mean."
Such a forthright answer dispels Buckley's strategy
so he reframes his question.

Ali looks at him again and firmly explains,
"I look at things in racial terms
because I *have* to look at things that way."

This reminded me of an incident Rob told me.
Ronbo was giving him a lift back to the city
after putting in a trade show in San Jose.
It was aisle-carpet night, the wee hours,
and they were stopped at the light—
a car full of big black guys and Rob, who is white,
in back, scrunched in between Otis and Mac.
Ronbo was at the wheel, Kenyatta next to him.

As they waited for the light to change
a squad car pulls alongside.
Rob, a bit of a joker, looks at the cops
and silently mouths, *Help me,*
a mocking twinkle in his imploring look.

Ronbo catches it in the mirror.
The light clicks green and the cops take off.
Ronbo sweeps his arm over the seat,
gives Rob a swift back of his hand,
then spells it out for him out as they get going,

"Everybody in this car got priors."

Rob says, sheepishly, "I'm sorry."

"It was funny, though," Ronbo admits.
Everybody laughs in relief.

The Moon Drew a Feather Across My Bones
for Cleve Jones

I came up out of Brooks Hall
the old convention center beneath Civic Auditorium
tired from working from six am until ten that night
into the Dan White riots

a police car was on fire
a long line of newspaper racks knocked over also on fire
the plaza full of protesters
culminating a candlelight vigil down Market Street from the Castro
to throng beneath City Hall, a gothic dome
that rose above the hostile crowd

Supervisor Diane Feinstein, elevated to mayor
by way of Moscone having been murdered
by Supervisor Dan White,
came out into a niche in the castle like a tiny doll,
our new queen, no doubt aghast at the spectacle
and the murders that had provoked it,
helpless above the scene below

I was afraid to go too far into the crowd
at first, hung more toward the back
but was gradually drawn in

a white guy blowing a whistle caught my attention,
he blew it urgently, as though exhorting the crowd
to shout and agitate whenever it quieted down,
he seemed apart from the demonstrators,
didn't seem gay, and when he saw me looking at him
darted away
I began to notice replicas of him, almost identical,
shifting throughout the crowd, blowing whistles
wherever the crowd grew quiet

I had the hunch
they were some sort of agitators
maybe hoping to incite enough violence
to justify unleashing the police

the incident in fact was not without casualties:
I read in the paper a few days later a policeman
took a brick in the nuts
and lost a testicle

the whole spectacle felt medieval
flickering shadows cutting apart the scene like a collage

above it the moon
witness to countless riots and atrocities in her time
hung splendidly
bestowing serene radiance
as she has done for millennia
calmly pulling ocean tides
back and forth over the earth like a black gown
the waves rising and lapsing as if the earth
were breathing in deep sleep
despite another violent nightmare.

I Can't Get Out of Bloomingdale's

I'm trying to live in the world
by being what I am
as a bear moves deeper into the hills
to get away from man

He might weigh eight hundred pounds
but you can't hear his footfall
pine needles spring back behind him
his nose alive to every trace
of man beast and flower

The trouble is I am a man
today I went through subway tunnels
where people sleep in dank smells
facing the wall
hands between drawn-up knees
inside ragged sleeping bags
practicing strategies of oblivion
under rotting clouds

The tunnels lead to turnstiles
that clank like jail doors opening
onto Bloomingdale's
a tidal pool that floods
at ten every morning

Doors open
we flow through
dissolute particles of stardust tossed
from the Big Bang into space
following waves of light

The perfume is suffocating
polished showcases reflect sentinels
of lipstick floors gleam
glassware sparkles . . .

In a casino of reflections
you take your chances

Overnight fingerprint thieves
wipe everything clean
erasing inner realms
a tyranny of surface prevails

The glass remembers us
in multiple reflections we slip from
by continuing to browse
but our faces catch up
always snapping back
into this insidious replicating fluid
flowing around mannequins that
catch our eye mock us
by not moving at second glance

During this spectacle an annoying
feeling of panoptic surveillance nags as we
reappear to disappear strolling
on a rolling wave among others
all looking to discover what we want
and hidden desires may indeed recognize us
light up our faces and lo!
we are not the shoppers but the shopped
factitiously aroused
by what we didn't know we wanted

The only way out's through the tunnel
and I along with everybody else
shove my groin into the exit turnstile
ignore that trifling indignity
to enter again where
those sleeping against the wall
anchor us in time

Buskers are playing
cello violin & flute
Beethoven at the gate
bottom of the escalator
as we ride toward a square opening
to the sky

Wheelchair at Mission Street Garage

He didn't last long on the corner
a black dude in a wheelchair
two stumps for legs, about the age
of a Vietnam vet, a big man
probably six four if he could stand—
pissed off, a volcanic island spitting fire
really fierce, and letting everyone
in the crosswalk know it.

Crowds at Fourth & Market eddied around him
glanced fearfully, his teeth

spat daylight across the street. People ducked.
Everyone knew he had good reason
but they had their own problems—no little cup
no witty sign no plea—just out there
letting you know what it was to wake up
in the streets, without legs.

There's a picture in the paper
Clinton shaking hands with the head of Vietnam
cutting a business deal
decades after the war.

Within three days they got him off the corner.
Some are left alone
if they beg within certain rules. This guy
was too much for the city's face
to face.

There's a hot thread
in each of us, a fissure of lava.
When it hits the sea it's a hiss
from the middle of the earth
for justice.

Hope's the dope that keeps you stuck.
Hope your disguise is on tight, hope
you won't lose what you've got
hope you'll be left alone if you just shut up.

The signal clicks, the light changes.
High heels, high-tech running shoes
dirt-blackened bare feet
step off the curb

blinders in place
suckered into the race
every man for himself.

Hard to Plan For

Outside the tire shop waiting room
a sparrow underneath a faded Subaru
sips from a puddle of condensation
dripped from the air conditioner.
Smoke from the fires is everywhere.

"Have a seat." The young woman
behind the counter takes care of business.
"I'll get 'em right on it."

The dude next to me into his phone
scrolls through pics with an expert thumb.
An older lady across from me
fidgeting with the clasp on her purse
looks at me, her face full of apology.
I smile and look away.

The tire shop is full of the smell of new tires.
We have Coffee Mate and hunting magazines
as we wait and are grateful to have made it
and not to be stuck on the side of the road.
I look out the window again.

The sparrow stays in the shade
under the bumper, her beak open for the heat
as if she's trying to sing.

River Fire
Grass Valley, 2021

After we were cleared to come back
we noticed burnt oak leaves,
caught in an updraft,
had floated to the deck, showing us
how close flames had come:
like shards of scripture on blackened parchment
we've been trying to translate, numbed out,
picking through the house and property.

The people we were
apparently left in a hurry, drawers half open,
dishes in the sink,
whole files pulled out of cabinets—
we went through this house trying to grab anything
we felt we couldn't live without, that called to us
while we could hear the hot wind in the high trees.

Death must suddenly show up
like that, us unprepared, snatching at our souls
flying around the room out of our bodies
like strips of celluloid flapping
free of old projectors
the movie screen gone blank.
We took off leaving any dignity behind.

Our house is still standing
with all the work it still needs,
my uncle's paintings, family pictures
too many to take, my books,
my wife's crystals . . . .

Sixty homes burned and my god the poor animals
one friend had ash-covered bear-cub prints
pawing her car to get in.

I opened up my computer to read
fires in Siberia were breaking records
burning more acreage
than all the world's fires put together.

Olympus in Greece, home
to the original games, burning.

Powder burns on our driveway
a flap of tarpaper torn off someone's burning roof
balanced on my gutter, like a scout
sizing up the place,
and going down the stairs leading to the lower deck
we look out on tinder-dry weeds. Blackberries
crawl through a visible layer of ash,
too slow to be seen moving, reluctant refugees,
lugging small dark-green leaves on their crablike canes
as if it's not too late.

O Romeo . . .
   —San Francisco, September, 2020

Hand me my armadillo mandolin.
I need to sing.
Turn on the Transporter Machine to the moment
shimmering alongside this one.
Somewhere wind is trailing a wake of sunlight
through a hillside of spring grass.
I see a sailboat leaning
under a bruised sky, so piercingly white
everybody's stopped on the Embarcadero
peering over their steering wheel
trying to remember where they were going.

The smoke hasn't gone away
this time, new fires are breaking out,
even in Oregon, and the fire season
is just beginning.
Ash flecks the cars, the leaves,
plumes of it, risen thirty thousand feet,
blocked out the sun, blocked the blue rays,
turned the air Martian orange.

In the City, fog darkens it even more,
streetlights still on. It's like midnight
at noon. In the East Bay the sun
is a small, orange disc, a demonic Eucharist
rising from the region of civil war,
to hang over the battlefield in the dawn haze,
weeds and crushed dandelions
beginning to lift, in hesitant, springing upticks,
to waver over the bodies. One soldier is propped up
leaning against a tree as if taking a break
jaw slack, mouth agape,
ants passing each other along his lips
as if along a windowsill, a man
in a 19th-century book, now come back to life

sitting on a chair, holding a cardboard sign
next to a crooked blue tent under the overpass.

The air knows what has happened,
the answer no longer blowing in the wind.
The smoke doesn't move.
We're so divided now, it's no wonder
civil war comes to mind. What can you do
in this bizarre light and toxic ash
but close the windows. Going out's as bad as staying in,
everybody contracted to whatever channel
profits by reinforcing their opinion.

Our indulgence of inertia killing the earth,
DMZ's everywhere, poetry a dandelion
in the divider strip.

That an atmosphere of war pervades this poem
is appropriate, people shot in the back by police,
most generals afraid to speak out,
dictatorship nearly in place.
Nobody's in control but a creep,
extolled as the Messiah by mostly good people
bewildered by neglect and damaged
self-esteem, when what's
really in control is the burning earth
and even now, I'm about to get in my car
drive across the bridge to meet someone
for coffee. We're all complicit
in this march toward global extinction.
Inertia is a motherfucker.

Going outside now, the news says,
is like smoking eight cigarettes.
We're a race of suicidal idiots
conditioned to band together in small groups
that circle each other warily, despise each other,
and we often don't even know why.
Perhaps we mistake this huddling for love.

Romeo and Juliet are dead,
having dared to love, having finally united
their feuding families, the Capulets
with the hated Montagues, in mutual grief,
by killing themselves.

Where does that leave us,
who are still in love, from different tribes, still alive,
and still needing fresh air.

The Circus Carriage, 1940
after Max Beckmann's painting

they have to live together
there's not enough room
the angry guy peeping over his newspaper
with a resentful glare
guarding something no one wants
maybe his helpless stoicism

the Tarot reader reclining like a courtesan in repose
a million miles away
looking right through you

the Mussolini-jawed lion tamer with his whip
sitting formally & stiff

the acrobat climbing a ladder
trying to escape through the roof

the dwarf carrying a lantern
a flame in it like a trapped canary

shadowy tigers in their black cage
tossing eyes like dice

it's a crash pad for circus performers
who have come to hate each other
but are stuck together
roaming a hostile planet
during war time
taking grim refuge in the color of the world
no one'll pay to come and see

Drought & Rembrandt

I remember similar winters in the seventies
without rain, the desolate expectation
drought causes in you, coming into the kitchen
a stiff dried-out sponge on the drainboard,
curved up at the corner.

One day I went to the de Young
to see a Rembrandt exhibit.
I recall a white lace collar
so intricately painted it sparkled like snow.
Glints of blue
flared in the gloom of a centuries-old painting.

When I came outside my eye was so alive
I was exhilarated by the sight of a fire hydrant,
rusty blisters peeling off dull red paint,
everything suddenly available. I felt restored
but more than ever aware
I walked under a spell
of fragile jubilance.

Stirring the Soup

A man in his kitchen
was stirring the soup
the faces rolling over
were simply mushrooms
passing through his mind
as he continued stirring

So long as I continue
I'm all right, he thought,
this wooden spoon is my oar
stirring what was and will be
since stirring the soup is
what is, stirring the soup
is what brings the rain

In fact it was raining
the cat sleeping on her cushion
below the window
a fire luffed in the fireplace
a procession of shadows
whispered in the chimney
shadows of flames
rustling robes
burning and leaving
their ashes

We look down on him from a hill
see him through his window in miniature
as he listened and stirred
fire turning pages of air
standing in his kitchen
where he belonged
but feeling uncertain
as if he were wearing himself, not completely
in himself

nearly small as a star among
so many windows
fused together by distance

We zoom in and the man enlarges
at the stove with his spoon
and we can hear a woman's voice

"You're still trying to get out of that car,"
she says. "It's been two months
and you're still somewhere else."

She knew that might seem abrupt, even cold
given what he'd been through
She felt he needed a jolt
and she was hopeful enough
to dare being playful. She extended her leg,
an eye for his attention, negligently
arched her foot backward, swiveling her ankle
to throw off his glance
were she lucky enough to provoke it

He continued to stir the soup
rays of the cat's fur spread apart
as it breathed in
closed again in shadow
when it breathed out
as it slept on its cushion

Rain pelted the window
Starlings sat in the eucalyptus
The mailbox leaned slightly
Rain poured off one end of a clogged gutter
and splashed onto the walk

The man continued stirring
the kitchen light on
the fire burning

It takes patience to withstand
the emancipating possibilities of insanity
he thought
The car was on fire
in the bridge tunnel, brightly lit
tile walls as in a shower
reflected flames

Passing cars were air
escaping the universe
fleeing or being sucked out

Fire was washing his car
he couldn't breathe out
so he couldn't take air in
the seat belt buckle was hot
the door softening
his face stretched

A monstrous black insect
unhooked the door, flames
flushed him out in an explosion of surf

He heard clicking
the insect knew what it was doing

He was being driven away, a mask on

When he breathed
it sounded like the ocean

Finally he said to her,
"It's not so easy
to get out of a burning car
even after you're out."

He knocked the long spoon
against the rim of the saucepan
and placed it cleanly in the spoon rest.
"I'm really glad you came over.
Let's eat."

Our Way Here
for Carolina Pezua

Photographed at the portal,
my arm in a negligent gesture on Inca stone
I see you now through a young lens
focused by an older mind

We felt our way through Machu Picchu,
lay in the meadow,
sat in nooks where people were tortured,
pondered the obelisk Inca tethered the sun to,
a center of the world
marked by a people who really believed the sun
would leave if they abandoned their ceremonies

I think of us at that high crag,
far below, the Urubamba river muffled by distance,
tumbling almost as quietly as our own blood
that runs so deep within us
we are the dream it carries,
peak-shredded mists
torn filaments,
our outer selves

I saw a courage rise within you
as you were drawn beyond my sight
over the edge of the sacred valley,
four thousand meters of terraced gardens,
full of weeds for the most part, but precise
channels incised into granite
by people without metal tools,
still trickling water to irrigate
the eastern slope of the Andes

"What the hell are you doing?"

"I am Inca," I heard you say.

It made me smile. I had to follow.
You descended the oblong stones
projected as a ladder at the ends of each terrace

without railings so your fanny
hovered over the abyss

You were oblivious of the drop,
thousands of feet,
it seemed to mean nothing to you.
A trance-like courage held you,
and I behind you, terrified I might end up
carrying your broken body
back to your parents in San Luis,
our civilized selves shredding like the rags of mist
in the *eyebrow of the jungle,* clear
and obscure in turns

It became our turn
to walk the wheel
beyond what we thought we were,
everything behind us that had lived and died,
leaving white granite
carved out for silver mirrors long since pilfered
in the Temple of the Moon
reappeared in quartz facets
fracturing moonlight into galaxies
we used to feed each other songs

Surrounded by work centuries silent,
heavy, imposed work,
several thousand meters of terraced
stones fitted without mortar, still so tight
you can't fit a pin between them,
forced work of anonymous lives
from tribes conquered by an empire that at least
allowed the wearing of tribal hats, preserving
that modicum of dignity, but nevertheless imposed
work for communal purpose beyond self,

leaving an empire's legacy in stone testifying
to unbelievable labor and vision,
created gardens the length of a mountain range
rising out of a valley, water sparkling
along exquisitely cut channels
now quenching weeds

We were each other's living link
to someone we'd been, refugees from civilization
who listened to the language of caves,
touched their Pleistocene hides as if placentae, who knows what,

together we faced earth again, on the east side
of the Andes, tectonic fangs
streaming clouds like beards of some Asian dragon,
lifting broad-shouldered people whose genetics
armed them with large lungs for the altitude,
who embodied contempt for fear of heights, disdained pain,
and whose descendants seemed to simply be waiting out
this curio of civilization

while the deeper, Incan one,
glows and dims like hot coals,
gets turned again,
promising a conflagration could tear loose
at a moment's notice,
a flag on fire, a furious tongue
born in the earth's core to culminate
in the cauldron of human dreams
to feed on current air—

We felt it in hillside fires burning outside Cuzco,
people drinking all day,
fed up, lines for rationed rice around the block,
the *solés* devalued overnight
until a riot broke out, and 16th- century
wooden doors, twenty feet high,
were shut and bolted, thin policemen
with pitiful .38s scrambled across

cobblestones to quell the sounds
rising from people invisible
in the darkness, hundreds of fires
like eyes on the hillsides, we inside
drinking cappuccinos, now listening
to feet on streets, yelling,
straps and slings jostling
—we looked to the waiters!
as if they were leaders,
protectors, but at least they were people
who had experienced this before
what will happen now
will happen only now . . . but it was just
an ember being turned by pain
a fork or two of flame
witnessed by two lovers on the brink
of an ancient world verging on upheaval
their own love resolving into a dream

Paso Huanquilla (Passing of the Moon)
—*for Abuelita, who waters the flowers*

Two instruments, a Peruvian *arpa*
a harp like a small wooden coffin
and a violin
wait against the wall with the musicians
for everyone to finish eating.

The harvest moon rises over the Andes,
over the village below.
Little Sophia expertly
passes out miniature eucalyptus canes
polished to an icy mahogany
by many hands before us
handles decorated by carved fingers that grip
the slender hammer in the middle
so we can tap
against a coin of wood for percussion.

She makes sure everyone
gets one, and her seriousness shows
she is a caretaker of the dance.
She has propped her cell phone on a chair
and is videoing the event.

Mirta's one-and-a-half-year-old baby, Yareli,
walks among us looking up,
her round face a small moon.

Abuelita, little Grammie, a hundred years old,
sits in her chair by the pillar
focused.

"Watch Miguel,"
Carolina advises me. "He knows the dance."
Miguel gently prods everybody into a circle
but I am too tall
and the clothesline must be taken down.

Eventually everybody's in position
and people start cautious, private steps.
As people walk the steep mountain paths
never fighting the mountain
they feel themselves lift as it rises
into this dance, each step a surrender.
Our blind, shuffling feet stir the dust
on the stone veranda with a wish,
a hush, a drummer's brush,
a whispering chorus.

This folk dance is formal, communal,
and something is understood
I can't escape being part of.
I remember folk-dancing class
in the fourth grade with Mrs. Brown
out near the tether poles.

I feel the value of tradition
even as I feel slightly comical, self-conscious,
to eventually revere how coherently all ages
attend the darkness.

The orange moon rising
from smoky clouds
breaks free to retrace steps in the sky
people may have forgotten
or disdained. *Paso Huanquilla*
is Quechua, and Carolina whispers
it started to make fun of the Spanish,
Quechua being the mother tongue of the village.
I footnote current colonial realities.

The circular music is entrancing.
Everybody is included and there are no stars,
although the grandfather, who doesn't feel well enough
to dance tonight, is whispered to be the best
and another grandfather who has died

could never be equaled by his sons or anyone else.
So there is a thinking back to those who have passed.

We quicken our stepping to start
raining our tiniest bones over the stones.
Our whispering, emphatic feet
echo in the valley like wings.

Going Where We Are

Driving back to the city
in Memorial Day traffic, passing
boats and trucks packed with vacation gear,
everybody heading back to work
after the three-day weekend,
sun burned, exhausted, hung over,
coming out of the heat of Sacramento Valley,
finally getting into the hills toward the bay,
dulled as the other nullified drivers
despite wonderful camping at the river,
I suddenly went on alert:

Two Great Danes loped onto the freeway barking,
scattering cars, forcing them to stop:
the dogs stood there, imperious, scornful,
the cars a flock of sheep, the dogs barking at them,
scolding them!
What they were! Magnificent.

An old woman stepped
into the middle of Park Presidio Boulevard
whirling her cane overhead
as if she were about to lasso a vehicle,
sending cars around her at odd angles, their drivers
terrified they might have to deal with her.

But I couldn't avoid her:
she stood right in my lane
and brought me to a stop eye to eye,
brought the rubber tip of her cane down firmly on my VW hood,
came around and got in. "Take me home," she said.
"Somebody stole my welfare check and my fingerprints."

She rolled out the whole story
on the way downtown to Eddy Street

to her Tenderloin hotel
where I left her off
in the bright sun.

I felt truly useful. For once
I was in the right place
at the right time.

I'd rented a VW bug in Quintana Roo
and was heading back to Cancun
after visiting Tulum. An old Mayan
stepped into the street
and brought me to a stop with his stick
no if-ands-or-buts about it.

He had a young woman with him
with a sick baby who was crying.
"Hospitale!" he commanded,
folded down the back of the seat
for the woman and baby
and took his place beside me.

"Andalé, muchacho! Hospitale!"

Listening to the Neighborhood

I'm at the helm on my back porch
totally in charge of nothing on Easter morning
but my coffee and the birdseed
I've scattered for sparrows
across the carport roof as I sit here
overlooking the parking lot
of the Vietnamese laundromat.

There's a great clamor and excitement
a festival feeling in the cool morning air
in front of the warehouse on the corner
as Mexicans, Salvadorans, Nicaraguans
break out pink and white ice cream carts
to pedal through the neighborhood ringing bells
to awaken flocks of shrieking children.

The sides of the El Tio Juan taco truck pulse
oompahs from tubas now at home in Mariachi
to declare music's democratic heart in Oakland's mix.

In the thirties El Tio Juan's taco truck
was Casper's hot dog cart, arrived like a covered wagon
from the Dust Bowl. Salsa has replaced ketchup
as America's favorite condiment. Recipes and instruments
are among what people carry dearly
fleeing war, following dreams.

Wary sparrows, eyes out for the cat
lounging in spring ivy climbing onto the carport roof,
hang back, perched
on the birch tree's dangling limbs
in a hierarchy known only to them
then chance it, splash down,
their sporadic pecking
pattering the plywood like beginning rain.

Corn kernels in the birdseed sparkle
the sun softly rising
people gathering below
line up at the truck for coffee
to take refuge in what's at hand—
the smell of sizzling chorizo—
to watch soccer on TV in the shade
under the awning as laundry spins.

A passing blue Mustang rapping rhyme
snaps along synapses dormant for years
setting off new neurons like a string of firecrackers
a bass line breaking in thunderous waves from speakers
so explosive the air shudders and Gospel soars
on the torn wings of an organ pumping out praise
because the storefront church across Foothill is open
receiving people dressed up for Easter—
dudes in sharp cream-colored suits
women's hats flouncing like fuchsias
patent leather shoes buffing concrete steps
as if shushing the celebrants
into the House of the Lord.

The couple in the parking lot
living out of their car
four or five days now,
having awakened slowly, attend
their toiletries. After he shaves
in the sideview mirror she seats herself
on a stool from somewhere
and allows him to comb her hair in the sun.

Dipping his comb into a bucket of water
he snaps off a whip of drops, lifts it aloft,
a baton between forefinger and thumb
conducting the entire spectacle
before drawing filaments of light

through the grain of her hair
—his movements sacramental
her chaste, expectant stillness
sustains a grace so silent
you can hear the 'hood sing.

just rain

dripping from the eaves
I thought it was her
walking down the hall

but she will never
come down the hall again

she put on raindrops for slippers
that would be just like her
letting me hear her

come down the hall once more

Trees in the Mist

shadowy figures
stand in air

one tree falling without moving
leaning so you know
that it is dying
but cannot be hurried

two people on the trail
outside the mist

in the illusory outside we cultivate
that difficult patience
of something dying, something
we are part of, *in the boat without cause,*
as Pessoa says, and pause,

to regard the mist in the ravine
momentary stillness
between what's happening
and what will happen

free to imagine
to remember the flying moss
in Ecuador, the moss that never lands,
how it shimmers and floats, constellates
jungle wetness . . .

and the elephants in the documentary
softly moving around one of their own
lying on its side in the dust
the lake drying up
in the expanding desert

the belly dancers
undulating, their sister in labor

screaming
giving painful birth
in the shack

and I detect in the synapse
we're leaping across
just standing here
the entrance
for us

into where something dying
or something being born
will not be rushed

appearing to disappear

as the boat's wake reaches shore
the stick bug sways
without volition
passive movement
part of its disguise
twigs stuck together rocked
by water its chance
to extend a leg
but careful to slack back
minutely timing
the illusion it's projecting
by choosing when
to be shoved
when
to take a step
that will betray
it's alive
it knows what eats it
can tell sticks that are dead
from those in the dance

The River Temple

To reap the benefit of repetition
we step carefully
down the tricky trail to the Bear
silently noticing
tiger lilies, poison oak, bay laurel, moss, mushrooms
living things that attend our pilgrimage

we talk over our lives
sometimes struggling to relinquish
whatever's separating from us
secure for a moment in our fragile pleasures
picnic goodies—hardboiled eggs
you wrapped carefully in blue napkins
cheeses, those organic herb-cured olives
from Peru, crackers, apples

in winter we see
hibernating ladybug colonies
unmoving at first but in which,
like little eyes, we eventually discern individuals
shifting position not quite
settled into the collective torpor

in summer red dragonflies
slide above the river on invisible wires
wings flickering an orange fringe

a sudsy light spiraling in the current
purls the galaxies
calming our anxieties, diminishing
our problems
drawing us from ourselves to ourselves
and each other

jellyfish

softly they pulse
luminous parachutes, a fringe
of red drops circling the body hem
trailing a gown
of mouths looking
like fallopian feathers
that often intertwine but never tangle

how jellies get along
move without regard
— pulse and drift
each pulse a propulsion
upside down
sideways, bump into each other
give way like balloons
without resistance, let alone
resentment

their lives are not careers
they constantly surrender
to current they hold being held
always going where they are
I don't even think they have eyes

these orange ones mesmerize me,
each a yolk
of filaments, occasionally
upside down, tentacles softly falling ropes
collapse
into the translucent chalice
they live in

little Lao Tsu's
leave me somehow
a little more free

how completely they drift
without knowing I exist
clouds of unknowing
offering a brief respite
from myself as I stand
in the dark aquarium
surrounded by other inhabited shadows
shuffling between luminous blue tanks

slack tide

is the only time
you can make it
from Alcatraz

boats in the bay
no longer align
with the tide, they drift

around anchor chains
like hands of a clock
that have slipped out of gear

the sea itself lapsed
aimless as a congregation
that has lost all faith

the gull on the buoy
doesn't fly away
as I swim by
filmed in his yellow eye

San Francisco Bay

For nine years I swam in this bay
nearly every day, all hours, all weather,
from Alcatraz, across the Golden Gate
diving off Fort Mason.
I always came out changed, sat in Ghirardelli's
overlooking where I swam
drinking a cappuccino on the outside deck,
blissful, but sobered by sorrowful calm.

I consult, almost scry, this surface,
green facets reflecting overcast sky.
I know it so well
how cold it is, how it tastes
less salty after spring rains
how it carried me on swims, lifted me,
forced me to fight currents
nudged me with the edge of its tide.

And all the while my swimming was really
an imagined conversation with my father,
who swam in this ocean as a young man,
and with whom I rarely talked
without arguing, things we couldn't say
to each other heard only by the sea.

Columbus Day

I remember swimming in Aquatic Park
coming out of the water still numb, pausing
on the way to the shower.

There was a small gathering at the shoreline
a news camera ready
to record something momentous.

A few feet offshore, a man of the street
by the looks of him, stood in a rowboat
his tweed coat sagging on his uneven shoulders.
He was supposed to be Columbus
coming ashore for the six o'clock news.

Some North Beach Italians with media connections
presumably descended from immigrants
were about to commemorate the great syphilitic navigator
by reenacting Columbus' discovery of America.

He seemed a little shaky
but stood ready to do his best.
They were talking him through it.
They'd even given him a helmet with a plume.

"Just act natural," the director said. "Ok,
now step out onto the sand."
He bent forward, a hand shaking toward the gunwale.
The boat rocked, an oarlock rattled, he faltered
and fell into the water. His helmet,
trailing its sad feather, spun beside him.

He looked up apologetically. In his red face
you could see all the things that had gone wrong in his life.
Regaining his feet he sloshed ashore,
his pants soaked, his sport jacket wet. A stagehand
handed him back his helmet.

Despite the mishap
the reporter still held the microphone up to him.
"Do you know where you are?" he asked.
The man couldn't answer.
It seemed a million things
were streaming through his mind.

"You've reached the New World,"
the interviewer offered. Some of the crew
were turning aside trying not to laugh.
It was a mild October day, no one on the beach
except me, shivering in my trunks and swimmer's cap.

Despite the cold, something about this American
vaudevillian skit made me feel obligated
to witness it to the end. Alcatraz floated dreamily
in the distance, softened by a white haze.

There were no Indians about
and we could all see
that Columbus was homeless.

At the Beach

Standing on a wooden bridge
a man and a woman
look into the clear lagoon below
Beyond them the empty beach expands,
darkened by last night's rain

They are solemn
Suddenly it seems
they have no future together
and so stand still, stunned into a brief truce with fate,
as if holding a bowl of water, filled to the brim
and not daring to move
for fear the other might disappear
A heron's taut neck,
just beyond them in the marsh grass
at the edge of the lagoon, poised like a whip,
holds time in abeyance

The railing dims and gleams, shadows
of clouds above the fog
shredding in the incoming wind
allow the sun a weak pulse

Holding each other, they take refuge
in the fragile nest of themselves
as they let go of lives they will never live

The Seahorse

While nuclear submarines nose between angles
of shadowy green in the South China Sea
where a new variety of seahorse was recently discovered, the stately
seahorse coils its tail around seaweed, a negligently
familiar gesture, and hovers
in a world where everything
sways. Steadied by that intimate touch, the rocking
seahorse stays in place.
Its hummingbird fins are a blur.

What does it know
hidden in the orchestral kelp
in its miniature G-clef body?

We answer its mystery with a category.
No seahorse knows it shows up in books
as a fish, and it doesn't know the strategic
geopolitical value of the South China Sea.

Its coherent eye is so meticulously
camouflaged by warping shadows
we cannot see it as it sees
through its disguise.

The seahorse is serenely alert
in its palace of kelp. Everything is perfect.

Can there ever be any natural thing we might contemplate
without reflecting mankind?

Thus my prayer for sanity is this:

The seahorse is calm
below the leaping ocean where wind
tears loose the hem of the waters
unraveling that magic carpet

coming apart in space
and coming together again so no one can tell.

Little flying horse of the sea
guide me through the trash
your eye wide-open, lift me
on the music your tiny wings make
without going anywhere.

Help me see how the theatrical world
choreographs so many dancers in disguise
without losing the beat.
Help me leave myself
behind, on purpose.
I'm behind on getting ahead.

Anyway teach me strategic withdrawal
to predict renewal.

Everything is dancing
to death and everything
is perfectly perfect. It couldn't be
any better than this.
There will never be any more that
than this, any more this
than that. The seahorse stays where it is
without saying a word
its wings going so fast
we have to imagine them
to see them at all.

temporary ongoing

a great blue heron flaps and lifts
from the estuary
where splintered pallets float
gathering the daily tide of wrappers and scum

the bird tilts
veers back over the freeway
fishing line hanging from its feet

to a cypress where it
luffs its wings
dances for footing, slightly
hampered by the monofilament

before settling onto branches
nodding under its weight
above East Bay commute traffic

neither of us can do anything
about the problem
but I'm the one with opposable thumbs

in the mix

swirling more slowly
in an inner tube
having just rippled below rapids where the river
widened into quieter water
I spun beneath alder trees
where damselflies were mating

males, attached behind each female's thorax
faced other attached males
seeming to shadow box each other
females holding onto blades of river grass
elbows jutting out, threadlike forearms angled
in a sure grip, anchoring their mates

wind high up the ravine
spilled down its path of paling leaves
lichens quivered on boulders
umbrella ferns twisted on their stems
ripples reached me
hair on my arms
leaned in the direction
the breeze was flowing

The River in Late Summer

in spring
cumulous clouds like molten pearls
tumbled up incandescent
into the bruised sky

the curtain strangely rising
on what was to come

now black oaks are already discarding their leaves
eaten into bits of crisp lace
some damp chamois-colored ones will stubbornly hang
motionless, like defeated prayer flags
in the mist of late autumn ravines

rivers slacken, scummy algae
cloud the bottom, putrid
water, dark as tea steeped too long
trapped in miniature granite tarns
reflects sky, a bluish cataract, in a sick
oily rainbow of decaying leaves

the river thins
exposing rocks like refugees
in the barren glare

raveling travel

he was talking about how it was
that a spider
found on different islands
separated by infinite water

could get around
undaunted by doubt

a silk thread
swept up by wind

maybe like a song
past understanding catches the ear
as if we could hear
filaments of ourselves on the air

a strand of dying sunlight
pulling thread out of a star

a more rational creature
would not dare
such a survival strategy

silk—unraveling
oneself—a form
of travel

Breathing on the Mobile

A mobile of gnats effervesces above the honeysuckle
every now and then one panics
and spins in a frenzy
like someone scratching a pen back and forth
trying to get it to write
knocking others out of orbit, jostling the swarm
that easily rebalances itself as if it were water

A formal mystery
that allows an individual to go crazy
while sustaining the coherence of the whole
that's always adjusting, inclusive, amoebic
to stay in the shifting shaft of light

A breeze quickens the flickering in the fountain
a swallowtail glides into the garden

I feel a thrill just sitting here
listening to insects, a range of sound
rising from the garden, many voices into one
teeming season taking shape

* * *

Alexander Calder discovered the mobile
while visiting Mondrian, modern art's
compass needle into the abstract patterns
underlying appearance. He moved
through Mondrian's austere apartment studio,
devoid of decoration as a monk's cell,
viewing rectangles of primary colors one after the other
focused as a bee, and finally said,
"I'd like to see them *move*"

An historical moment
that hangs above countless baby cribs
reconciling time and space

* * *

Aeolus gave Odysseus a little bag of wind
to help him on his journey home. Almost there,
unwilling to trust the helm to anyone else,
Odysseus fell asleep at the tiller, exhausted

His men were jealous and resented him
for hoarding all the gold and gifts he'd received
from their adventures, in which everyone had risked his life,
and some died, gifts then stored below deck in holds
filled with casks of sweet wine, bronze spears,
pearls, goblets, fine tunics—so the men themselves
were coming home empty-handed

In their mutinous mood they undid the silver strings
and opened the little bag of wind
while Odysseus slept, released Aeolus' winds
all at once, raising such a storm it threw
the ship back across the sea
putting them through still more trials

More men died, skewered and eaten by Cyclops,
others turned into swine
while their minds remained human,
and Odysseus himself, compelled
to enter Hades to seek the seer Tiresias
for advice on how to proceed,
met shade after shade
in the region of the dead, including his mother
who disappeared every time he tried to embrace her

* * *

Everyone is given a little bag of wind
to get home. Some open it
and hear their voice
twist and expand like murmuring birds

Others squander the winds they've been given
spill them into the world all at once
then spin in chaotic frustration

I caution myself to sit still
feel the wind's full range
within me without doing anything
except trying to cultivate that difficult patience
it takes to see that merely breathing
moves the swarm over the honeysuckle

Ol' Republic

a local brewery
next to a small-engine repair shop
a few benches outside
upside down wine barrels for tables
everything wet, cloudy sky
whitening like a pearl

the sun won't break through
it's already five o'clock
I sit outside drinking a beer
look at the straight trees in the windless sky
treetops silent . . . legions of them
imagine what they've witnessed

feeling good after the gym
next to other people hanging out
dogs patiently content on cold concrete
spongy air—

when out of nowhere
a determined wind emerges from the trees
like the ghost of an exiled grizzly bear
wet leaves flip across the parking lot like frogs
following it

a dog's nose quivers
but it's not worth lifting his head
people shift uncertainly
talking and smoking
reinforcing their circle

the day picked up a little speed
nudged the hammock of our afternoon
into evening, a slight chill, a ripple
still passing through us

as we rise and fall in the wake
of what has happened

the state flag with the grizzly on it
hangs damp and limp
over the gas station across the street

timing my breathing

I stepped out of the car into the fragrant shade
of a flourishing fig tree
growing just beyond the bank parking lot,
spared by a property line when the bank was built,
its scent buoyed me on such lucid memories
for a second I wasn't sure where I was

five years old
stretching to reach the hot doornail
at the chicken coop door, knees bumped
against the pail of corn as I snapped the nail loose
and pushed open the wire gate
squawking chickens gave way in a wave

the purple figs were softening and warm
sandpapery leaves, sparkling with fine grit,
brushed across the dry shingles of the coop,
a sweet aroma of corn rose from my bucket
and light softened on the dusty quince next to the fence . . .

kernels rattled as I poured them into the trough
when a gray rat appeared with unblinking eyes
at its hole in the dirt, its pelt plush as velours, saw me
then disappeared like a popped bubble.
I dropped the bucket, but before I could run
felt myself in a shimmering mirage
black heat curls above asphalt roiling toward me
from a diesel truck idling
at the drive-through ATM

when its moist, warm exhaust reached my face
I held my breath
the air of my childhood a dream

We Heard You Singing
for G & C

We heard you singing in the other room
as we were looking at the ocean
wind shaking the bushes
that looked like they wanted to come in
the sailboat might have been a buoy
or the buoy was a sailboat that leaned
we listened to you singing in the other room

You were getting Charles ready for the day
since he's blind now, and Lowry
was playing his Irish fiddle as whitecaps
were coming to shore
we looked at the ocean while you sang
gliding in the canoe of your voice
singing from the other room

the sailboat angled like a butterfly
so far away it could have been a buoy
bushes shook in the wind, Lowry's lively
fiddle spun a wheel and the kettle whistled
the old dog groaned
three white pelicans flew in a line
over the slate blue sea

you sang, the fiddle played, the kettle whistled
the sailboat leaned or if it was a buoy
chimed beyond hearing rocked by the waves
currents made stretch marks in the sea
we watched the ocean, the kettle was ready
but we felt the moment private and went out for coffee
we heard you singing from the other room

Premonition in Spring

I don't know what lifted me away
maybe cherry blossoms nudged loose
in sporadic flights
but slowly I realized
at a small outside table
I was in a gentle vortex
centering something so tentative
yet certain as an incoming tide
I felt balanced on my chair
no heavier than a leaf

Defiant trees tossing manes on the hillside
displayed every shade of green
although winter chill still clung under the overhang
so I was glad for the slice of sunlight on the ledge
where I rested my arm
everything within promising to resolve
in the cohering motion of the coming warmth

The couple behind me whispering
an intimate stream in a foreign language
swelling and lapsing with the trees
uplifting and paling
on the modulating winds of early spring

A man lifting off
widening to touch
shores beyond reach
disappearing in his breath
someone scattering his ashes
from a sea cliff at Pt. Reyes

Fall Squirrels

Squirrels speak in little sentences
over and over, six or seven
squeaky revolutions,
it's like they're trying to crank up a Model T
that shivers, sputters whistles and stops
over and over—there's nothing to do
but take a breath
on the brink of anxious despair
and try again
in the fall silence.

The squirrels
bicker helplessly, like people
revolution after revolution an effort
little squeaks in each tremor
they try to get the engine going
the engine of language
not even knowing what it would sound like
not even knowing what it would do
just driven to try and get through
to break the silence
that drives the squirrels to the edge of hysteria.

So they try again
squeaky little sentences
over and over
to no avail . . . the engine of language
hasn't even been invented yet.

But they can't give up
they are surrounded by quiet
winter coming on
mist in the ravines
doesn't move
there's no way
to get away, no way

to say what they are trying
to say.

The animals are cold
knowing what's coming
and nearly out of their minds
because they'll never have enough
acorns.

Although the squirrels' situation is dire
we have to admire
their determination
the incessant pleading
in their urgent squeaky sentences
and how touchingly
they tuck their agile black-gloved fingers
to their chests as if about
to receive communion

and squeak, even daring
at times, to bark—tiny belligerent barks
coughing forth puffs of fog, like smoke signals
in protest, or in appeal.

We try and the squirrels try
over and over
to get an engine
to turn over that won't.

They bicker and
chase each other like smoke up the tree
then chatter at each other
and we watch them
they're like comedians
who won't get off the stage.

It's vaudeville all over again.
It happens every winter
as the earth dies in our mouths.

Geese

I thought for a second they were bowling pins
balanced on the bank of the drained reservoir
but they were so attentive
radiating a devout aura, a congregation
of little monks robed in light
soaking in the last rays of the sun
their brown-hued breasts
filling with the day's last warmth—
about twelve of them.

We didn't think we'd disturb them
since they seemed far enough away
on the opposite shore
but one started working the rusty hinge of his voice

and they all gently took to the air, flying as one fabric
layering the valley with trombones
spiraling higher as they circled the reservoir
passing above us, lifting just enough
to thread an opening in the trees.

But what if we had been more patient
crouched on our haunches
in the shadows at the base of the trail
and attended the last light with them
felt the coolness come, the darkness, and when
they took off, unable to fully see them,
listened to their wings
as they swept overhead and escaped
with that part of ourselves
no one can see.

Spiders

When I'm wasting time
it helps me to look at them
this one just hangs there, upside down
below the lamp
a daddy longlegs
patient as a galaxy
as if it has all eternity
to wait for its prey   Sometimes, though,
one waits so long it dies
hanging in its untidy strands

Idly glancing over
I see through them and realize
they've gone, legs folded
little closed umbrellas
a bit hideous how they silently
evaporate, in the corner
of the bathroom window where
they took all
their chances

The windowsill
is The Altar of What Has Fallen,
littered with specks of spider crap, a wing
floating a rainbow, a bent thread a leg
a nano knot in it
that's a marvelous knee
discarded in the serene dust

Who can keep up
with spiders   Once I cleared
everything out of my office
washed it down and painted it
Within hours a spider appeared on the ceiling
the paint not even dry

I read that no matter where you are
you're within twelve feet of a spider
even on Mt. Everest
where the Himalayan jumping spider lives

Eight eyes orbit its head
giving it 360-degree vision   Supposedly nothing
lives up there but this spider   It eats insects
blown off-course, drifted too high,
like transmigrated souls rising
on wings stolen from previous lives,
incomplete beings, destined
to become food for this spider
that survives the cold under a thin layer of warmth
hovering on rocks of the world's highest mountain—
thin as our atmosphere relative to the globe,
like a layer of saran wrap around a basketball
according to scientists

But just look into the face
of one of these little jumping ones around here,

wolf spiders, I think they're called,
with four eyes, the beautiful orange

black and white face
takes you back a bit   It sees you
with such cunning, unhesitating intelligence
you realize it could *take* you

as in high school
when you might be caught absent-mindedly
staring at some kid, not even seeing him,
a tough kid, and suddenly he says,
What're you lookin' at?

That snaps you out of it
You look away slightly bewildered,

even embarrassed, wondering,
what *were* you looking at

The jolt of fear helps you focus   Absent-minded looking
isn't seeing   but what if someone wasting time
is really a cloud of unknowing
like a man at the railing of a ship, seeing by unseeing,
facing the sea
feeling the wind
feeling his face
knowing something of the limbic zones we travel

If I died in this chair
they'd use my body
for tie-down points

I'm not really wasting time
I'm looking at this spider

April Seventh

The sun is making the camellia leaves
sparkle and I've got a decent cup of coffee at my elbow
as I type along in bed. I will get up to do
whatever I want to do; I am healthy;
my financial anxieties are in abeyance.

That the world is turning on a spear
through its beautiful heart, that blue jays
tune their shrieks by sharpening their beaks
on a whetstone of human bone
indicates the wider world is continuing
its common suffering under a calm sky. I suffer the silent
opening of the white camellia in private bliss.

trumpet player

a shadowy figure
leans against the overpass support
out of the rain, playing his trumpet
his open instrument case
lies empty on the sidewalk
too far away to be serious . . .

cars go by in the rain
shrouds of inertia —

it has to be the most hopeless sidewalk
for foot traffic
but maybe that misses the point

you cannot see his face
so deep inside his hood
it may not even be there
he plays to the applause
of sizzling tires

his mouthpiece just touches
the cave from which he blows
music into the atmosphere
—a draft from space with a tune in it
echoes under rumbling concrete—

perfect acoustics

The Old Man in the Plaza

I'm an old man now
sitting like a movie extra
in a blocked-off street faire
full of sunscreen tents and outdoor seating,
bales of hay imposing safe-distance barriers against Covid,
reading, as it happens, Salmon Rushdie's story,
"The Old Man in the Piazza."

I'm delighted by the phrase,
"the vanity of certainty"
a vanity the old man in the story falls into,
unexpectedly, because he has led
a life disciplined by hermetical practice.

I read for ecstatic flights
swept out of myself while sitting in a chair,
in a coy town surrounded by a culture
of cutthroats and cannibals.

The old man in the story, it turns out,
cannot escape his buried longing to belong.
Sensing this the villagers exalt him,
make him a judge, so strong
is their desire to be told what to do.
They honor him so much
he begins to believe he is truly wise and,
worse, useful. The recluse becomes another
ordinary person, so compromised
we turn away from him,
recognizing ourselves.

I look up from the story and careless
laughing teenage girls
step to the curb from the puddled street
rippling a reflection of the old bank
now a pastry shop with faux doric columns.

The gorgeous insolence
in their laughter makes the world
shimmer like the apparition it is.

kalimba of weeds

long stemmed dandelions
bouncing in the meadow

the weight
of a single bee pulling
down each stem
letting go

a field of springing keys
playing a melody

rising from the field
soundless as dawn—
a death song

a feeling spread through me like water
the bees playing flower after flower
going extinct
still singing

An October Cricket Posts a Personals Ad

I saw you at the kitchen window
listening to the space between us
forgive my forlorn sound, a single cricket
at this time of year
but this is our only opportunity
I know you hear me
there are so few of us now

in August there were too many of us
you *couldn't* hear me

we sizzled like a field on fire
waves within waves every voice
conjuring for a listener

the solitude we feel now, the few of us
still singing
has a stranger allure   our songs
no longer overwhelm the quiet
they are as much listening as singing

a raven's wings scissor the air
over the meadow
Schubert is playing from the other room
as you stand at the window
he would understand this silence
we listen into

come outside
my legs sing
feel the hair on your arms rise and lean
with the wind following
my violin into late fall ravines
where the mist subdues the sound of traffic
beyond the trees
those who sing in October

sing to enliven your cold cheek
evoke a frosty plume, a gasp . . .

answer me

we stand within a terrible pause
my brethren are dead
disappearing beyond memory
glaciers so fragile a cricket
cracks them loose with his song

let's enkindle between us
in the space between species
what we're afraid to hope for   let's sing
as stars shake a raiment over this
temporary immensity   call me
however you can   I will hear you

ABOUT THE AUTHOR

Long active in the San Francisco Bay Area poetry scene, Gene Berson holds an MA in English literature from San Francisco State University. He has taught poetry workshops under the auspices of SFSU's Pegasus Program (which eventually became California Poets in the Schools) in everything from one-room Wyoming schoolhouses to reform schools, Indian reservations, and as a high school teacher in Oakland. Gene is the author of *raveling travel* (Open Book Press, 2019). His poems have appeared in *American Poetry Review, Bastard Angel*, and others. He worked in the trade show industry (Sign Display Union, Local 510) and was a translator in Korea (7th Infantry Division). Gene grew up in the Bay Area and currently lives in the foothills of Northern California with his wife Ruby.

HIP POCKET PRESS MISSION STATEMENT

It is our belief that the arts are the embodiment of the soul of a culture, that the promotion of writers and artists is essential if our current culture, with its emphasis on media and provocative outcomes, is to have a chance to develop that inner voice and ear that expresses and listens to beauty. Toward that end, Hip Pocket Press will continue to search out and discover poets and writers whose voices can give us a clearer understanding of ourselves and of the culture which defines us.

OTHER BOOKS FROM HIP POCKET PRESS

Poems from the Threshold: Charles Entrekin (poetry)

Café Dissertation: D. James Smith (poetry)

Storyland: Keith Dunlap (poetry)

The Occasionist: Curt Anderson (poetry)

Jester: Grace Marie Grafton (poetry)

The Berkeley Poets Cooperative: A History of the Times:
　Charles Entrekin, Editor (essays)

Even That Indigo: John Smith (poetry)

Ex Vivo (Out of the Living Body): Kirsten Casey (poetry)

The More Difficult Beauty: Molly Fisk (poetry)

Yuba Flows: Kirsten Casey, Gary Cooke, Cheryl Dumesnil, Judy Halebsky,
　Iven Lourie, & Scott Young; Gail Rudd Entrekin, Editor (poetry)

Songs for a Teenage Nomad: Kim Culbertson (young adult fiction)

Truth Be Told: Tom Farber (epigrams)

Sierra Songs & Descants: Poetry & Prose of the Sierra:
　Gail Rudd Entrekin, Editor

A Common Ancestor: Marilee Richards (poetry)

Terrain: Dan Bellm, Molly Fisk, Forrest Hamer (poetry)

You Notice the Body: Gail Rudd Entrekin (poetry)

WEB PUBLICATIONS

Canary, a Literary Journal of the Environmental Crisis:
　Gail Rudd Entrekin, Editor

Sisyphus, Essays on Language, Culture & the Arts:
　Charles Entrekin, Heidi Varian & Luke Wallin, Editors